Marsupial Mouth Movements

George Kalamaras

Červená Barva Press
Somerville, Massachusetts

Červená Barva Press
P.O. Box 440357
W. Somerville, MA 02144-3222

www.cervenabarvapress.com

Bookstore: www.thelostbookshelf.com

Cover art: "The Mammals of Australia, The Tasmanian Tiger" by Gerard Krefft (1871)

Cover design: William J. Kelle

ISBN: 978-1-9500-63-30-7

Library of Congress Control Number: 2019953263

ALSO BY GEORGE KALAMARAS

POETRY

We Slept the Animal: Letters from the American West (2021)

Luminous in the Owl's Rib (2019)

That Moment of Wept (2018)

The Hermit's Way of Being Human (2015)

The Mining Camps of the Mouth (2012)

Kingdom of Throat-Stuck Luck (2011)

Symposium on the Body's Left Side (2011)

Your Own Ox-Head Mask as Proof (2010)

The Recumbent Galaxy (2010) (with Alvaro Cardona-Hine)

Something Beautiful Is Always Wearing the Trees (2009)
(with paintings by Alvaro Cardona-Hine)

The Scathering Sound (2009)

Gold Carp Jack Fruit Mirrors (2008)

Even the Java Sparrows Call Your Hair (2004)

Borders My Bent Toward (2003)

The Theory and Function of Mangoes (2000)

Beneath the Breath (1988)

Heart Without End (1986)

CRITICISM

Reclaiming the Tacit Dimension: Symbolic Form in the Rhetoric of Silence (1994)

ACKNOWLEDGMENTS

I want to thank the editors of the following magazines and anthologies in which all of the poems in this book, or their previous versions, first appeared:

Action, Yes: "Marsupial Mouth Movements"

Alphabetum (Greece): "Many Great Heroes"

Arsenic Lobster: "The Color of Darkness," "The Age of Bent Blood in the Throat," and "Forest Hermit Sutra"

The Bitter Oleander: "The Sincerity of Fire," "Milkmouth and Dissolve," "Gold," "Too Much of Me," "King Me," "Moth Milk," and "Gobi Noon"

Calibanonline: "Blood Hook," "Almost Autumn," "A Pitiless Expanse," "Bathtub Oils and Historical Bones," "The Blood of the Poet," "Mantra Diksha," and "The Methods of Production"

Clade Song: "Their Names and Ears Had Been Erased," "To Consider Our Milk," and "No Here but Now"

Combo: "Great and Awful and Gifts Us"

Dispatches from the Poetry Wars: "The Naked Length" and "Retracted Order"

Flying Island: "Left-Handed Practice"

Forklift, Ohio: "Moon Thrashings" and "Where Might My Sacred and My Most?"

Ghost Town: "Great Thirst," "She Bent Over in Her Tight Black Slip," and "An Impossible Immediate Self"

Heart of the Rat: An Anthology (Willow Springs Books): "A Plague Rat Carrying Calamity Becomes a Panic-Making Horse"

International Gallerie: A Journal of Ideas (Mumbai, India): "Tying the Traveling Man to the Tree of Soul"

Kenyon Review Online: "Water Museum"

Luna: "Already-Breathed Air"

Map Points: "My Allotted Value"

Phantom Limb: "Less Than or Equal To," "Tapeworms," "Wasp Work," and "Seven Minutes, Twenty-Three Seconds"

RealPoetik: "Corymbs" and "But I Never Would"

Redactions: "Which Hemisphere"

The Refined Savage Poetry Review: "That Said"

Salamander: "The Book of Perfect Hygiene"

Sawbuck: "A Dependent Compassion for Your Scar"
Segue: "Angora"
Starfish: "Rasa"
SurVision: "Starlight in the Deaf Man's Ear"
Talisman: "On the Way Out of the Body," "The Diplomacy of
    Apples," "Death of Death The," "Scar-Light," "A Once-
    Flourishing Pain," "Our Smallest, Most Tender Selves," "Ever
    Broken," and "Buffalo Jump"
They Will Sew the Blue Sail: "Placental Chauvinism"
Word for/Word: "Thirteen," "My Not-Yet-Young," "Shamanic
    Meltdown," and "There, There"

Three poems also appeared in *Book 1* of the *Illuminated Book Project*
(Editor, Brian Lucas): "Page Two," "The Practice of Sleep," and
"Longing in the Grand Grassland"

I also want to thank the following for reprinting some of the
preceding poems:

The Bitter Oleander: "Angora"
Verse Daily: "The Age of Bent Blood in the Throat"
    (October 3, 2007)
Stockport Flats (in the chapbook, *Something Beautiful Is Always
    Wearing the Trees*, 2009): "Marsupial Mouth Movements"
Ugly Duckling Presse (in the chapbook, *Your Own Ox-Head Mask as
    Proof*, 2010): "Buffalo Jump"

I want to thank my wife, Mary Ann Cain, for her unending
inspiration and support. It is such a gift to share our lives, work,
and love. I'm also immensely grateful to John Bradley for our years
of friendship and for his thoughtful commentary on my poems,
none of which would be the same without his attention and all we
share. I also owe tremendous gratitude for the friendship and
continual support of Eric Baus, Dan Gerber, Ray Gonzalez, Juan
Felipe Herrera, Patrick Lawler, John Olson, Paul B. Roth,
Lawrence R. Smith, and Tony Trigilio. Huge thanks to my former
poetry teachers—Philip Appleman, Don Byrd, Mary Crow, Judith
Johnson, Roger Mitchell, and Bill Tremblay—for nurturing me in
my formative years on the poetic path. Sam Hyde of Hyde
Brothers, Booksellers in Fort Wayne deserves thanks as well—for

giving me a refuge (mostly after store hours!) and for providing stimulating conversation and an unending supply of great books. Gratitude must certainly go to the animals that populate these pages—for living with such openness and presence—especially the thylacine, the name of which, in Greek, refers to the "dog-headed pouched one." None of these poems would be possible without the yogis of India and the mountain hermits of China—past and present—whose quiet contemplation continuously nourishes my life.

*for Benjamin—the last known marsupial
wolf (d. September 7, 1936)—and for all the
thylacines that came before*

*and for anyone who, at one time or another, has
longed for the primordial pulsings of the pouch*

TABLE OF CONTENTS

The Naked Length

Parasites Without Which the Swan Would Die

Shamanic Meltdown

Bathtub Oils and Historical Bones

A Dependent Compassion for Your Scar

It is not uncommon for the age of young marsupials to be recorded, not from the date of their birth, but from their independence from the pouch.
—Robert Paddle

. . . majesty for whoever falls from the clay to the universe
—César Vallejo

Marsupial Mouth Movements

The Naked Length

Starlight in the Deaf Man's Ear

I lay among the camels, bathing in the soft blue starlight of another
   dawn.
Not *another* dawn but the Mongolian rain in my belly.

It was like the story of pulling the Golden Lotus Woman's
   corpse from the angry river.
We will place a good strong stone in our mouth and pretend the
   crimson hue.

So many lives I've lived, like being the younger brother of Rubén
   Darío.
Nicaraguan bloodletting from my pharmaceutical cup.

Or when someone named Simone made sounds into my mouth, as
   she guided my hand across her voluptuous thigh, teaching me
   the words *belly-blur* and *please*.
And that time I only lived three days, thirteen hours, four minutes,
   thirty-seven seconds, refusing suck at the unwed breast of a
   Malaccan dawn.

Dear Book of Precision, Dear Book of How to Win a Mongolian Pony Race,
   tell me how many times have I taken to The Steppes, fearing the
   Tartars in the barbaric encampment of my soul?
Tell me which lives I've led with dignity or blame.

That time I awoke not as a baby but as epinastic enzymes in the
   afterbirth of a camel foal.
There are herds that pass through me—as I write, as I sip the
   hot morning hoosh—yawnking and spitting the dawn down
   from dark to a deep dampening blue.

Page Two

I must begin again, turn over a new grief.
Sometimes I get very quiet and dream I have no shoes.

All those time-tested cave walls, and still I can't properly read rain?
I am not Chinese, not the fourteenth century, not a goldfinch from
  Japan.

I lived half a century in the pouch of a pygmy possum, in the belly
  of a Greek wooden horse.
All my grandparents' superstitions hindered me like splintered
  ribs.

When my insides bled, that's precisely what they were supposed to
  do to keep the platelets clean.
I asked her why she slept each night beside a raccoon, whether it
  was to learn the dissolve of collapsing one's bones nightly
  onto the sheets.

Everything now is moist, as if it had just rained or bled.
What I'd like most is to remember the flood and pieces of my
  name strewn across the torn, blowing grass tufts—the list of
  insects on the second page of every book ever bitten.

The Color of Darkness

I'm going to begin by imitating the bones of broken words.
Ask about my hair, and I will pass you the dictionary, marked at
    passages for *rain-soaked*, *decipher*, and *shelterbelt*.

It is easier to roast Yukon Gold potatoes than to divvy up my
    mouth.
Part of you has already slid slantwise into my throat.

I can expect at least one of your eyes to stay fixed in my pocket.
I've kept it imprinted on a mirror with the lid of the compact
    closed.

I once meditated with and then asked a Hindu swami in Banaras
    the color of darkness.
He described washing his robes in the Ganges and suddenly leaving
    his body for hours at a time.

Angora

That seemed deceptively simple.
The lines were fixed as eight or more ways of mouth.

My teacher said, *Conditions are always neutral.*
There is a line of mind on which we swell.

I have heard of Bihar village folk granting naked Jain monks a
   bath of hands.
I have heard the refrigerator recharge its cold belch in the night.

I wish I could describe what it was like, that life, to live in China's
   mountains those years as a panda.
No one would ever believe a paper clip could arm wrestle a staple
   gun.

We inherit our wandering black and white selves like we inherit
   these bodies, one action at a time, each inscribed in the astral
   spine.
How else could I have ever thought up on my own all these
   years of hair?

That's one reason I salivate whenever I touch angora.
I keep recalling what it felt like to be lost.

Moon Thrashings

I could feel the hustle-bustle of many years of defeat.
They measured my uneven ears, had decided upon pearled barley
    for the stew.

I went about scraping sleet from serapes and the new thrashing
    nets.
A resigned umbrella poised rat-like—drenched but content.

When we watch a person sob, needles sew our lips shut as a single
    whingeing moon.
We walk out onto the heath in fog, wringing our hands.

Who are you to cover my sadness with ash?
Have our bones blurred? The blood flea escaped? Into whose
    mouth and how?

Please, if a stranger breaks his arm, don't befriend him just to tell
    him of my emotional hurt.
Don't remind him of the time stars bit my chest, shirring and
    slurred. Sunflower-fierce and damp. Sunflower-fierce and gone.

Blood Hook

Snow crows convulse my dignity for the length of rain.
An incessant bed insists the contour of rotten apples.

It's raining so hard the beards of cypresses serve perplexed welts of
    moth time.
Thousands of dark limps struggle-swage my heat.

I am convinced that a stalk of celery is a great loss.
The lush continent is a shade of universal adamancy.

He collected coral snakes, and she kept a tortoise named Gaston.
In those days, I often wondered who would polish his eighty-year-
    old shell if he was to outlive his people.

Once again I dream the new house with secret rooms.
Floors *between* floors smell of Kundalini's slow resin as it hag-hairs
    between chakras.

I held your wrist and heard the blood hook tear from a remarkable
    little bone.
Don't mistake my desire for bird beaks in your chest.

I saw you again today in that wool skirt and sweater.
The depth of your breath—its abundant rise and fall—suggests
    thousands of lengths of dark rain.

The Sincerity of Fire

Incidentally, it hurts.
I was sequencing a settling of crows, adoring my most intimate
    suffering.

When mountains approach, there's beauty in the dire, wild chives.
We rarely trust anything except the three voices of descent.

We barely hear all we have lost. The strength of it and clutch.
We imagine the first rib and how it must have felt to sleep that
    deeply.

It seems the unripe fish inhabits the hammer *and* the lamp.
It's not that profound to detect plum birds in the many whirls in
    your hand, electric currents of the emu in the dropped leaves
    of the brain.

The days are lengthening even as they shorten, are the foraging
    haul of the trapped dead.
For any nesting fox guarding its coat, at least three willow branches
    in Iowa shrivel unsaid.

There are deadfalls of a stormy vowel striking my hand. Holding
    me captioned.
The lame hear nothing, it appears, and the certainty of my words
    in a helium balloon sincerely burns away.

Many Great Heroes

There were many great heroes of the Greek War of Independence.
Fierce men like Odysseus Andhroutsos and Theodoros
    Kolokotronis.

Sometimes, when I gargle, I imagine lions cleansing their teeth on
    the jawbone of a zebra.
Living and dying are not black and white, not as simple as hunger
    fulfilled.

I recognize all that sticks to me, even the rib resin of others.
That's one reason I rarely eat in front of people—I don't want to
    absorb from them more than I can safely crave.

I keep the ash of an asparagus spear in a small locket, tucked inside
    a shirt.
I never want to forget what it was like to be yanked, body-smart,
    from the earth.

The struggle for freedom from Ottoman oppression is not a
    metaphor, my immigrant grandparents not an idea.
I still feel blessed to be here, yet, like any good Greek,
    superstitious—even leery—about having my bones secretly
    removed one night while I sleep. Their passion cracked. Their
    puff of smoke duly deported.

Left-Handed Practice

It is raining, and the blood bloat immortalizes Hikmet and Desnos.
Late at night, my empty hand longs for fervent sleep-talk.

I am a resewn flock of geese breaking winter fence weight.
Her cry in my mouth. Her terrible terrible calm.

When I investigated the color green, all I could detect were
    hundreds of wood ticks grumbling the flesh.
When I implored the bowl of dead fish, their one dead eye was a
    crisscross of silver and gray thorn.

Nazim Hikmet made the prison yard in Ankara almost dark
    compared to his inner traps.
Where, ultimately, *was* the voice of Robert Desnos, and what
    pleasure might it rain-ache?

Now I am sure I must have always been left-handed.
I wrote this, deliberately, three times with my right.

Less Than or Equal To

Please, do not look sad. Do not sumac-stem my brow.
Truly, such incarnate salt implicates the coxcomb of my name.

Because I don't fully rain, some pungent bean curd is fierce.
Of the six lingering warmths, the seventh and eighth are most
    calm.

On a precise pear leaf, fresh forms of water modulate my mouth.
Look at the brown tiles of the moon as an enormous hereditary
    mistake.

When my grandfather broke water, he gave birth to a revolver.
Because I have wondered about the gas lamp, he has stayed dead a
    long time.

Once, I planted sunflower seeds in the chest of a percent stranger.
She was mathematically part woman, part lampshade, part
    frankincense. I was torn between three halves of self-hypnosis.

I once read that I spoke possum shoals while everyone else
    advanced backwards through pouch-ponds of rippling
    moonlight.
A marsupial nervous system is, after all, more isolated than the
    aqueducts of a plant.

Behind the owl-toped ridge, a sapphire of bloated noon burns like
    sunrise at sea in its *setting* at sea.
Yes, all time happens at once. Do not look, please. Do not my sad.
    The word *strange* is somehow less than or equal to *an enabler of*
    huge sufferings, a bad case of the bends.

Thirteen

We sat beneath the giant baobab, dreaming of African ash.
Fraximus was sacred to the Norse. Now a constant rectitude is the
   live fruit of a she-oak.

The belly-burns made me think I'd once been a horse.
That's one reason I always wear either black or brown—they
   protect me from the urge of your spur.

Lemon coconut cake is a way of planting soybean breathing into
   the chest of a crow, here across the great ocean?
One plus one plus one equals nothing—or perhaps a steadfast
   dissolving of salt?

I discovered I had a blister after nearly sixty-five years and hope it
   doesn't disappear.
It's weird—even screwy—to see my childhood fears reflected now
   in its gravelly, riverbed stance.

Was Kabir ever colloquial? Was Rumi? Hafiz?
When either heard the clock strike thirteen, did they crow-talk?
   Rewind their words? Did they suddenly want to die?

The Naked Length

Thus, one of us reminisced the distant Gandhi years.
Another, the demise of *Wani*, Japan's Crocodile School of post-war
poetry.

A third said nothing but went to a field, revolving his body beneath
a surplice of stars.
There was no fourth, except the heretics of pantheist grass.

That night, like all others, was dark.
From the alphabet tripod, the upstream grasp of a deadly fish.

All I ever wanted was love, is how I'd recorded it in my diary a decade
before.
It suddenly reappeared as bosk rills in the messy hair-matted sink.

A piece of a thirty-six hour glacier was undertaken for study.
Men with pipes listened to radio accounts of Calcutta floods.

They spent their days aboard a Swedish steamer searching for the
Northwest Passage to Yokohama.
They spent nine months of ice bartering with the Chukchi locals
for a bride.

The sea froze. Meerschaum became a manner of breathing, a spate
of seasonal release.
Mendelssohn remained in their beards the way reptile eggs might
hide a sigh.

Across the radio waves, a Bengali mapmaker experiences the
drainage of all his cardamom tea.
A dog in a sand bed near the Ganges might suddenly sneeze.

We scratch our ear, bite ourselves silly, pocket-lint our hands as a
sign of fate.
Celestial harmonics present many openings, thrash this tail or that,
say Japanese Dada *meant* something.

What does winter have to do with the naked length of my
beloved's body?
What waited for us, a radio-breath away, at the end of the world?

Tapeworms

For far too long I tamed tapeworms, taught them a steady path of
lambs.
I stood in the doorframe of an owl and welcomed my loss of a
loving throat.

Someone gave birth to an egg. From its center sprang an epistolary
braid.
I wrote my shame over and again in the remarkable anthill of a
blood orange.

All kinds of sea creatures direct my age.
She wore a pencil skirt, cruel as a crupper.

A charmable puff of smoke formed directly in the connective
tissue of gnats.
We passed the membrane bone and inhaled deeply thereof.

Honor thy honey badger and thy hookah, it is inscribed, slantwise, in the
thorax.
Forsake all manner of snug settlings, and seek to inherit a yurt.

Tent-like, I covered my mouth with a moist of hands.
Some ached, some strained my secret name, and some contained
shreds of rich green staph.

When she released her bodice, she could once again breathe.
We discussed the complexity of parasites, salt pork, and hands.

For far too long, I have raised tapeworms, distributed them as
redemptive—if not disturbing—seeds.
They helped each person eat him- or herself clear through, from
inside out, from inside *in*.

Parasites Without Which the Swan Would Die

Water Museum

The water museum opened yesterday.
All those crystalline forays from here to there.

There was a stopwatch with Argentinean sun-glint from the time
of Magellan.
There was a compass from a Japanese schooner that refused to
point north.

A Chinese junk kept lugging young women from Bangkok into
white slavery.
Penguin skins beached on Java as if even primordial love wasn't
enough.

Conquistadors camped by the fountain of Peruvian bloodbaths.
Dip your finger here, and cross yourself three times to ward off
the teeth of a moray eel.

Do you want to learn a prayer?
Try absorbing the banana splash of waves in Fiji refusing the
constabulary and its men.

The water museum closed today, as if Antony had never wed
Cleopatra, had never drunk horse urine along the Nile to
demonstrate his strength.
Blackened, disparate, hopeless, nautical lines of bacteria invaded
the Cape of Good Hope, dispersed as blackwater fever,
elephantiasis, a malarial shivering for more.

Look—there are the throat gullies of the trumpet swan.
And there—the parasites without which the swan would die.

The Practice of Sleep

Train switch, as if in my chest.
An emergency of water founded on the principle of sleep.

Let all the machines step gray across the imagined bellybutton of a
  possum.
Let me play myself dead, as if I'd never stretched my birthmark to
  release owl resin throughout my strain.

A nocturnal journey has nothing to do with a Romanesque oar?
We were slaves to our emotions, and we rowed ourselves silly,
  trying to determine the blind depths of our past.

Where does the speech sound, and how might the absent navel of
  a marsupial relax?
Where does the forced tongue? Where might the soft pallet of my
  mouth if I could only and was and fit?

I'll admit it. We gave everything human away just to study Japanese
  Surrealism within its proper cultural context.
I ate sushi every day and found light bulbs in bathtubs, and one
  dead fish, as I recited my line, time and again, the way it *should*
  sound if I could but unclearly speak my sleep.

The Age of Bent Blood in the Throat

When the ithic gods wagered words, we had an enigmatic release.
I carried the flower of her voice in my thorax like bent iron.

The age of short skirts. Liniment seed on all that bleeds.
It was a tireless trace of gunpowder on my finger. Or some stain
    just as veined.

I sat with her for coffee and almost slow hair.
We talked of a disturbing black gill at the bottom of the world
    pumping its enormous pain.

It is more comfort to nuzzle a secured suspicion.
It is calculated saliva in the boats of dark gravy.

Sure, she spoke of underarm stubble that required shaving.
She told me that her name, backwards, spelled *Only Your Mouth*.

All right. I know I can say something born.
The terrible cities extended coast to coast and spoke our mutual
    weakness like safe hands almost holding—below the
    table—everything we might regret.

Great Thirst

Having entered the forest hermitage, our bodies sensed the coming
   of the Boer War.
Our bones remembered the Orange Free State, how it had hurt to
   boil human blood.

One of us got bit by a black fly, which produced great thirst.
Now we can recognize any dogma, convinced that surrender is
   sensible hope.

A broad blue womb, delirious with elephant flesh, has severe bone
   structure.
We sat in a corridor of bandages and wept our heads.

By eleven years old, I had already developed a delicate and shy
   psalm.
I would arrive less angry than organ music across cool blue marble.

Tonight, I will revolve and allow the crease of your curried wing.
I will fold your lips like pocket lint I keep deciphering for a potent
   smile.

Listen. We arrive again and again, afraid of how far we've already
   come.
We examine our hands and assure the ends of the earth.

I'm not quite sure a simple knife wound is even intended to pass
   through the ocean slope of a shoulder.
While solving the color red, you take the long snout of the boarfish
   as a prize.

Almost Autumn

Once, when the insouciant leech was lifted from the bedsore, we
 praised the estuaries of the five senses.
I dreamt of the hairy patriarch of everyone's calm demise. And we
 were alive.

Then there was the horoscope containing nine secret lives.
Each, somehow, belonged to me.

It is further from my left hand to my right than from my right to
 the left.
I don't know why, though I scent of it and tongue and speak.

Yarrow clots are stalking the blood.
A hawk in moonlight is an enormous measurement of breath.

Another success is inevitable.
She sewed the button, and I felt closed in—almost connived—in
 the not-quite fall.

Boil water. Shred rags to filter the coffee. Sop the rain-soaked ache.
Help me to see the world.

Tying the Traveling Man to the Tree of Soul

To be frank, it scared me to consider cradling the skull.
We approached the skeletal tree with shamanic respect.

Someone cut a finger on this moon or that.
A woman in brown corduroys bent into my ever-bending blur.

Lord knows she was gorgeous.
The horns say ivory comes at a great cost.

Like the buttocks with its single cleft, I am split between good and
    more good.
Everything is in balance, even the sky of her eyes, respect for her
    color-blood.

Give me your hair. Wear it Egyptian. Say you are an ancient way.
Every knot in it is a string tied to the end of what we can never
    know.

To be honest, I was growing less and less honest.
What I mean by this is that I knew I was staring at my own
    bleached-bone skull.

Sure, the skull was smiling. Yes, it gave a grimace. The string said,
    Not this, not that.
Each morning when I wake, broken parts of me remain drenched
    with the wet of the moon's milk.

My Not-Yet-Young

Having a biotic reaction, I was everything I might live.
I will never forget driving into town, unable to see the winding
    white lines in rays of binding sunset.

No one knows the weakness of a rope-burned *was*.
We smell feathers of migrating geese and appear enrapt with a
    quixotic *said* and *done*.

When all's diminished, expect no incident of bored fish.
Sure, everything married everything else, and ordinary leaves did
    not become a windy routine.

I tried extravagant arrivals and late-night winter almanacs.
Everyone agreed I should learn to fly and protect my not-yet-
    young.

If I wake full of oxygen, will you humiliate my breathing by
    investigating why?
What if a hovel of thrown stones, containing both the birth and
    death dates of paramecia, became my repeated need?

Corymbs

Of the various favorable tendencies, none is more important than
    sound.
We will make another crying life, tongue by electrical tongue.

We will every day. We will poetry and its source.
Who will mouth the burning shoals of all that hair?

Who will burro-walk the cliff face with the foreknowledge of the
    riverous salve of a braid?
We climbed the skeletal structure of a rare breeding bird.

We could not hear our own story.
We were convinced we could never requiem our ash.

One kilometer away, a tremendous tornado spiked three pours of
    quite milky silt.
It has now been several days, but the first set of words somehow
    measured my mouth.

This judgment, I confess, cannot account for the rough sound of a
    scream.
That, too, is music, and the ordinariness of replacing our tongues
    with remnants of aloe suggests how many scars I had to star-
    solve just to stay alive.

My Allotted Value

Once the practitioner attains calm, all the sores are gone.
It's amazing, really, the way I might speak with your mouth.

Your fear is that you are not a solitary *I*.
You examine the intestine of a musk ox, try to decode the imprint
    of the galaxy of bees that maintains the scar of your birth.

I refused to eat the world, a revolving that brought both of us to
    willow root in the spine.
Even a soft-spoken shoe, no doubt, could compose a learned
    sleeve.

I dreamt of a ferry passage to what had been Ceylon.
I visited the supposed graves of Cain and Abel.

I touched the jawbone of an ass.
I refused to cut my shoulder-length strength.

Now you ask my name, and all I can do is shudder as if it truly
    belonged to no one.
Your grave intestinal hair might more belong to a wraith belly or a
    worm.

In terms of the examination, my allotted value is a possible
    absolute.
To attain the notes of the Japanese koto, I have had to—raccoon-
    like—continually collapse my bones to enter the Milky Way
    mirrored in mud puddles by the grate.

On the Way Out of the Body

First, on the way out of the body, look back upon small talk as a
    host enthusiasm.
Ask every severe wish be granted at the lamasery in Kounbourn.

The following day, we devoted every detail to eating precisely half a
    carrot.
If you eat it, the monk had said, *it will no longer be just half.*

Every day passed like snowed-in shepherd pace.
We dispatched modest papers, but who forgot the precaution of
    a fixed ceremony, and where were the lambs?

I began to contemplate the periodic use of commas.
I assumed the necessity to pause, over and again, like inhabiting a
    new body, birth to birth.

If rhetoric instigates the ulceration of canker sores, then speak to
    me melodically but only when I eat.
Remember, it's all right to precipitate yourself in the name of a
    sudden seize of rain.

By which I mean that the trail, without snowshoes, was long.
By which I mean, in the body or out, we hunt for questions and
    exclamations.

Retracted Order

The occultists sought to organize the Bulgarian working class.
Though proletariat, I was totally singed to the letters of their
    middle names.

I could never exact their stance.
I wanted meditation. I wanted Patanjali's *Yoga Sutras*, the laboratory
    of the spine.

Still, what comes to a basic secret tried to regret itself.
I know the fork of lifetimes, of ideological facts located in
    meanderings in the palm.

After not mentioning death, a biography of the Czar was the worst
    kind of river flower.
I kept smelling for my nose, helping myself to lungfuls of dead,
    pre-established air.

If you are confused, insert some transient brilliance in retracted
    order.
Witness for yourself the old patterns and necessities of events.

Circumambulate the cold cobra eggs. Hitch their unhatched
    tongues to the moist of the spine.
Any nest will do, as long as it faces east.

I tried to delimit the extent of my elbow, which pretended to be
    smoke-tree slosh and its magnificent branch.
The certainty of this description captured a scritch of music,
    inner-most and moist, with great alarm.

A Pitiless Expanse

Or perhaps the upper indigo edge of a volcano.
Or perhaps an ancestral pain in my expression of laminated
    watercress.

I no longer know the layers of snow, nor multiples of three.
If they contain fire, that too is uncertain.

How quiet the clicked religion of everyone's film-stripped youth.
How grave one of the many unmarked ant mounds of Lorca.

I was told all this by the sound of a brick fireplace resembling
    mantra diksha in my right ear.
It was the winter solstice, and the radio was suddenly agape with
    Brahms.

Or perhaps it was the hibernation cough of a bear. Hookworm in
    the nonexistent stool.
Perhaps it was liver, sautéed Nametoko bear livers to be exact.

This issue, having departed from the layers of snow, was a pitiless
    expanse.
I thought of numerous other expanses—sparrow breath of spun
    wool, the retina of a dead giraffe, that narcotic mole in the
    bellybutton of a certain woman.

Then I returned to the study of bones, not the least of which was a
    brightly failed corpse.
It was sure, finally, of its emotional density, of unnamed fire, the
    untamed transience of all that human weight.

Milkmouth and Dissolve

Lost now among the Milky Way breathing of your words.
I write with a pet squid, *The rest of our mouths resides in the tongue.*

We exhale parts of other people we have inherited, back out into
the plants.
We all know from where they come—those qualities of good silk
and bad.

Each time I speak, there is a guttural elongation of light.
We approached clumps of sassafras root as we bowed before the
plate.

He wore oatmeal mornings all the way to work.
Women vowed never again to marry if something—God forbid—
were to unexpectedly claim their pet hamster.

We cannot stop floating through one another.
Treat this extraction of chthonic bees from your throat with the
tender swelling of joints.

We rasp upon and split. We milkmouth and dissolve.
We had left our tongues, one by one, in the openings we had not
known would exist.

Shamanic Meltdown

Longing in the Grand Grassland

I awoke once again in the amber autumn of vast Mongolian grass.
Horses secured me, huddling my wind with matutinal fire.

The women rose early to make a milky breakfast and collapse the
    tents.
All my memory erased, I slowly grew to fear death.

Oh, the full moon is caught again in a green bottle.
What comes in threes can surely always survive.

Somewhere, it is north and south at once.
I wish I could eat a snowberry that would not infect the intestinal
    complexities of my breath.

Each birth, every *moment* of birth, an infant feels sunrise demise.
    The weather is pale, anemic-green.
It was as if she stepped out of a bee swarm, handing me an egg
    with both her name and mine inscribed inside.

Boswellia grew there, under the linden discovery of perfect breath.
The ponies are most secure in their milky Mongolian sweat.

If a man be born summarizing sassafras.
If he recognizes the many movements of the moon.

The Nankeen kestrel perches itself, exposed to the many snows.
Like other Australian birds, like mouths on fire, it has no clear path
    of migration or moons of the most molts.

The Diplomacy of Apples

Dormer windows slowly assume any possibility of light.
Thousands of stars in my body give the appearance of a peony-
    bent, dawn rain.

So I've decided to strain my life toward the sound of moist for
    less?
So a long time from now I might pick sea lice from the pouch of
    badger blood and remove the fishhook from my most-human,
    childhurt ear?

The time to love could be the world.
Multiple discourses collide like philosophies of rain.

I realize I come from the sound of worms scraping across the
    diplomacy of an apple.
What awful, what pain we release just through proximity and
    wrath.

Treaties were signed. Treaties were broken.
Hanging from the dawn-breaking tree outside my window,
    incantations of not-quite bandit bloat blur the bathroom mirror
    with the feed-sack strain of my name.

Wasp Work

They brought the cufflinks, one after the other, and still I counted
    to twenty-nine.
I remembered the Manchurian ponies slaughtered in bites of South
    Pole wind.

When I paid no special warning, I remained in strict voice time.
Confused acquaintances threw power horses into my real or
    imagined candidacy.

Before daybreak, I heard whispers of hurricanes fried in mud slosh
    and butter.
I could not imagine the usual pan, only oil-drenched recitations of
    prayers.

One after the other, my thoughts kept pinning me to myself, I to
    me.
So much human strain remained at the rim of an untongued
    buttonhole.

At least once, the auguries prefigured our weather of false praise.
Earnestly, our bedclothes were consistently creased, as if we'd
    never lived outside the body's reach.

Let me say it this way. Wasps worked the length of lacerated
    longing.
They knew the secret fluids, the sacral hive, from whence this
    stinging came.

She Bent Over in Her Tight Black Slip

Our tongues, too, had been cut—just below—at the frenum.
Some saliva or other was always wagging loose.

We knew every tendon of everyone else's body.
It wasn't from studying nudes in drawing class.

When we lay long against one another, we heard an eye socket
    shift, the tragus of the ear open and clothe.
We heard a drizzle of bee's blood penetrate the pillow.

Someone called for rinse water.
There were only two of us in the room. She bent over in her tight
    black slip, which made the sad of me nervous, craving her
    weight.

I lay myself lengthwise across every particle of her enlightened
    groin-dust.
We were red-crowned cranes avoiding the iron content of the river
    bottom. The hesitancy of the dance.

Did I know her the way I knew the constants of my mouth?
We were giving birth to one another's fear. Time and time again.

Gold

Then there was the exchange of saliva for blood.
The Word said *re-create*, and we had our fun.

Or tried to.
What we touched in the other's rib was mud resin upon which the
    hen-eel had shed slivered impressions.

We move to and fro in the exaggerated motion of underwater
    speech.
We try on a name, short life to short life, before we become
    beautiful.

The trees are wearing what had once been a shirt.
The penetrating red of a totemic flame tree of Thika takes the
    deutzia bush's strange compass of snow back toward the color
    green.

Moan resin drops from the sky during each full moon.
We grow hair and grovel and grifted with.

Come with me into my lip. Past, present, fierce—like a jangling
    coin.
Bite hard for gold. Bite hard for gold. Try to make me bleed.

Shamanic Meltdown

The Siberian shaman appears flute-like in his recompense.
I know his ecstatic toad like I know the ice shelf to which he is
    impacted.

The *College English* article said something about *socio-epistemic demise*.
There are marmots with a deeper sense of pedagogy.

Sometimes when I take vitamin E, I imagine a second skin of
    walrus blubber protecting me.
Yes, I feel naked, especially when you eye me while peeling the
    skin of a blood orange.

I heard the shamanic sound like an ontological meltdown.
The Peruvian shaman had come to Fort Wayne and had given me
    maca the year before to heal the inflammation.

If I fail to breathe.
If I knew your name.

Sure, we grow up and in doing so sometimes crack the thatch,
    moving far from the hut.
When he shook his maraca and sang to me and scoured my pain-
    body, I knew I'd never again be the same.

Too Much of Me

Dogs, like fierce maracas, become part of our knowing.
We might shake the seeds loose but still sigh ourselves into a deep,
twitching sleep.

I'm trying this lifetime not to be a blood pheasant.
I'm a loner and meant nothing when I wrote you, except, *Did we
listen to the identical thinning of bees?*

Before listening to Brahms, I revitalize the sound of my every
internal organ.
I give up yesterday's wants, balanced precariously on an empty feed
sack.

Whose patron died in 765 C.E.?
Would we even respect his verse had he not left Chengdu,
afterwards, to float his way down the Yangtze?

I am trying not to be a panda again, a timber wolf in the next life, a
shred of embroidered silk.
Should I stop inscribing bees into the still-smoldering entrails of a
caterpillar?

The idea was to make things *right* this time.
Too much of me keeps flooding back, weeping, like a person not
yet cured of birth.

There, There

I have needlessly complicated the presence of a bone.
I am at a loss, the dogs are confused, and the tightly knit social
fabric of my ribs appears disrupted.

In the dirt before me, certain as I stand, the bone.
I know that if I found it, it must have secretly come from me.

But why the wind this March morning, growling as if not quite
through biting me with winter?
Hasn't it chewed us enough, and are we not better for having
stayed three months indoors?

I have retreated and hermit-sat.
I have investigated the great migrations of the musk ox, the
exasperated bees that ride the spiny crags of the long intestine
and get shit out, buzzing, miles from their hive.

I am not trying to say that's how I feel.
I am not convinced I have come without a purpose.

Still, the constant, the marrow mewling from within, asking for
milk words this time to scrawl away the loss.
Even the dogs are confused when I hand them the bone and—
patting them—confide, *There, there—there is more, there* will *be
more.*

Death of Death The

Say it fast, and you'll sense breath go out of the breath.
Say it backwards, and *death of death the* makes little sense.

It was agreed upon that we would share the *thikana*—our common
abode—dividing up the Indian feudal state accordingly.
Heaven adopted earth, and earth adopted actual words.

They arranged themselves on paper and called me *Grandfather Rose*.
I referred to them tenderly as, *Be still, my child*.

You are sick and tired of all my talk?
You wish I'd fall through all that sad and emerge never again to
speak?

The frustration the furnace feels with the summer is more than
competition.
The mouth says, *No need to bring me the hose—I'm perfectly content in the
cage of my craving*.

All right. I'll confess. It wasn't the exposed water pipe, after the
plumber knocked out the wall, that got me.
It wasn't the moon, wholly broken, its urge-turned dirt and
underground pools.

Something is always bending toward me, full of unquiet milk.
I used to think it was the pouch of a marsupial wolf. Or a worm
farm from Tasmania on fire.

Where Might My Sacred and My Most?

It began with a displacement of bones.
I started to scratch with my left knee, then my nose, and realized
my sleep was again acting up.

If I exhumed my face, would Picasso place me in one of Cornell's
tiny boxes?
If I ate too much cashew butter, would my slowed bowel recall
childhood picnics without watermelon?

I swim in an eel-infected tea and never reach an approximation of
my ear.
I kiss everything electrical and crave all things Bengali, particularly
the widening bight of the Bay.

If a pint of ale stood as a cable relaying insinuated grief, would you
know I was Sagittarian?
If you saw my collection of rare poetry magazines, which ones
would you connive—close-mouthed—to eat?

The chronic lightfall through stunted sycamores offers me an
exclusion of mouths.
As if the tongue might get shucked-off, diphthongs were
disallowed.

Where might my sacred and my most, and how might its size?
If I died several more times before you were born, would you love
me without knowing me, or simply find value in one day hosting
my blood?

Their Names and Ears Had Been Erased

Yes, the sacred sash of eels keeps bleeding its mark across my
    forehead.
I am shunned as if I'd never truly been a fish.

There was the delicate feast, the bush fires near Mombasa ineffably
    cool.
There was the soon-to-be-plunged, the horizon of an amazing
    locust.

Give me an injection of morphine and say you're sorry for avoiding
    the task of mending a shirt.
Say you're sorry for not recognizing my mouth or the ear cleaners,
    on a Bombay street, going deep.

When they brought the paper, no one knew why their names and
    ears had been erased.
Mumbai was sometimes Bombay. Banaras sometimes Varanasi.

One of us swore it had to do with a previous birth.
We couldn't remember whether we'd been able to afford a coin to
    close the eye.

Everyone was misunderstood by everyone else, which meant we
    were not fish at all.
The electric tongue of some marvelous eel offered to swallow me
    chakra by chakra and mark me toward dissolve.

What was I doing when I'd devoted that one entire life to tending
    an anonymous tree?
I'd become a gardener, obsessed with Backflower and Ash, and
    would not allow a single rib to be cut or branch to be burned or
    broken.

King Me

We are composed primarily of one another's echoes of pain.
Witness the copperhead coiling into itself as if reflecting the
    moon's worm.

Once again the passing herds make an unbearable rain.
I knew my weather, and was certain of yours, but could not
    recognize your transfiguration of salt.

You brought me the book. It contained nothing but verbs, the
    language families of trees.
Some letters were chewed by bookworms, though we knew them
    as eels, so past and present intermixed.

Sometimes I find you in your sleep when I least respect it.
We leave the body, float through the silk of one another's thorax,
    and play a game of checkers on the back of a hippopotamus.

Then it's time to bathe, and she descends her powerful back into
    the slosh of the Zambezi.
How long will we hold on as she takes us through the flavorful
    reeds?

You love the cool but lament the loss of the checkers, you tell me,
    as they float downstream near the crocodile's thrash.
A simple game of life and death, you say. And of getting kinged.

The Book of Perfect Hygiene

Make me the copper sun of Golgotha, the shivering of the sperm
    whale just after mating.
Make me the coupling link cuffing your shirt, one of a pair, as if the
    length of the left arm is not distinct from the right.

The Tantrikas know that left-handed practice is not dirty.
In *The Book of Substitute Flesh*, it is written that we will douse one
    another's owl with saliva-spill and maps of kerosene.

Which is to say, isn't the memory of topographic ants more than a
    fierce itching?
Which is to say, the Romanian lightning bug begs to be swallowed
    so that it might harmlessly x-ray the lower folds?

Make me the crush of a temple bell mending the morning air with
    melancholy.
Make me the attitude of the many-shirted, of the morning mist
    damp with moon maps to an unidentified other.

Which is to say that left-handed practice is not dirty, was never
    really dirty.
Which is to write our names over and again into *The Book of
    Idiomatic Demise*.

In *The Book of Perfect Hygiene*, staphylococci linger on the eyelash,
    lovingly grazing the belly hair with brutal butterfly kisses.
It is written over and over into our flesh that—for a short time—
    we are alive.

Bathtub Oils and Historical Bones

Forest Hermit Sutra

Then it was time to read bone-bleed from the fortieth Sutra.
It simply stated the condition of the dead.

Many came from all over.
Even the forest hermits paid their emaciated respects.

Part of my scar is something achingly beautiful.
Yes, I'd been a child. Then a man younger than I'd been at age
    four.

I don't walk in a way that easily ripens my mouth.
Summer-slush the cuts of my tongue. Kiss them to speak.

I gave myself to the solitude of a word. Retreated to the hermit
    cave of a marsupial pouch.
It was warm there. Nocturnal. I could take suck. Close to the belly
    of the mother, inside of which whirred the world.

Placental Chauvinism

There was thick bracken lining the trail.
We heard vocalizations in the darkness all around, hiss-like coughs
  and barks we feared came from inside us.

Wet sedgeland and buttongrass plains were a most exciting
  surrogate.
Ultimately, it's worth remembering that many trees were clearfelled
  for what we took as progress.

Tasmanian tiger or marsupial wolf. I would have loved you even
  had you not died out.
Some part of me is always misnamed, trapped by feckless
  ignorance, hemmed in by creepers, eucalyptus, and giant trees of
  stupidity.

So it was that not just mammals but plants found domestication in
  Mesopotamia around 8,000 B.C.E.
So it was that across the great ocean, Tasmania became cut off
  from the world.

Starving convicts fed pigs scraps from passing whaleboats.
The pork, they said, began to taste of seawater and lamp oil.

So it was that the marsupial wolf—the thylacine—got blamed for
  thousands of dead sheep.
So to have a placenta among the King Billy pines, beech, and
  blackheart sassafras was thought to grant access to the
  Darwinian throne.

I have been down on my knees far too long, searching for the crisp
  of my lost tongue.
If I had a pouch. If I had four tiny embryos clinging inside. If I felt
  their suck at my milk and their vulnerable hiding from the world.

Limb by limb we grow, even in sleep, twitching ourselves into a
  minute nervous system.
Replete with the disease of so many former lives, we once again
  enter the world.

Have I come this time with a predilection for vascular tissue,
   hunger for the hibernating bandicoot, the terrestrial mountain
   shrimp? A taste for the internal organs of the spiritually soaked?
This coughing bark. This thick and bracken and trail. This certain
   uncertain coming unto the world.

Scar-Light

There is little doubt that I am constituted of scar-light carried in
    the astral spine, like torn tissue, birth to birth.
She wore green gaspeite set in silver, discovered in Australia when
    mining for something else entirely.

I could be a hushed bastard, and sort of was, wandering decades
    through the Urals and Carpathians, searching for my father in
    wolf scat and dens.
Then I found the unusual small influence of the phrase, *So say I*
unto our mouth.

When pretending to be a dagger, it is important to hide in the stew
    until the last possible moment.
The psychoanalysis of an egg has been shown to expose a dignified
    filth.

Who is ultimately in the best position to be a dog?
On what sofa might we sleep? And what deep twitching would we
    dream?

Moth Milk

I don't think I have fully grasped the blood of your beauty mark.
I've seen rouge on your cheek, yes. I've even seen your monthly
    caress of a shed egg.

In the birth of a horse, every grace is unconditional and complete.
But I sometimes don't appreciate the cocoon of moth milk in
    which I am wrapped, how it protects me from evening feasts of
    bats.

You've offered me a trip to Canada, how I could see for myself the
    coming of the Iroquois, the migrations of every wingèd thing.
You've offered me time, explained that I could return to 1785, to
    horse-blanket trade and the worship of a luna cough.

Whose authenticity would you accept if I was inclined to apologize
    for a weak argument of wings?
Would it be Breton's? Daumal's? That of Henri Michaux invoking
    the swampy dark of Daniel Boone's heart?

There's a sign beneath my foot, as if a ghost lamp approached
    from below.
It might be Paul Delvaux or the empty face of one of his multiplied
    brides.

The last time I played with blood, I blamed you for not completing
    your marrow.
This monthly birth of good and bad, this *this* and *that*, has left me
    hatchet-red, authentic in the way I accept myself, antennae-
    tough, moth milk and all.

Which Hemisphere

If a house is built precisely on the equatorial line, is it in the
　　hemisphere of fathers or mothers? Placentals or marsupials?
I saw a bird fly into the mail carrier's ear and nearly knock him
　　over before spreading Florida through his bones.

We might donate profits of our pain to the Rimbaud Museum.
He's the reason for the plenitude of Ethiopian coffee in Europe,
　　though his tale of gunrunning was more mythic.

Some jittery thing has worked its way back into my life.
I flinch when my wife cuts uncooked butternut squash by banging
　　it, cleaver in its chest, against the counter.

I am not afraid of my lack of public craving.
I wear it as one might wear previously unfinished pants.

One leg at a time is the best way to climb the stairs.
When you get to the top, nothing is as it appears.

After the initial compliment of a self-sacrificing nap, they played
　　cards until everyone had lost.
As to the occupants of my invisible whaleboat, we outlawed guns,
　　and an attack of terrible dust frightened us all from across the
　　great water.

Seven Minutes, Twenty-Three Seconds

I stood there, that life, weeping for lack of a good pocket hanky
    and any compassionate glance.
They'd disemboweled me in the courtyard, made me watch them
    burn my own entrails, there, before I died.

I do not exaggerate. I am not the mouth of a louse.
I wore a wig, I recall, like a newly shouldered barrister.

You say that's one reason I cannot easily make decisions this time?
You imagine me a judge, not a barrister, complicating their court?

Throw that in with having once been a photographer at the burn of
    an Algerian century, with serving toast, cleaning latrines a
    century before in Bombay and Tashkent.
Somehow, the smell belonged to me.

No, I don't recall every birth.
My coffee voice is too numerous to equalize the sad of the
    waitress's glance.

I remember, though, what it was like to watch my insides burn for
    the longest seven minutes, twenty-three seconds of my life.
That's one reason I imagine holding most every hurt person I meet.

That Said

That said, don't get discouraged.
The Country of Eight Islands is somehow shallow yet firm.

Do both of our scars resemble?
If we rubbed them together, in a secret place, would starlight
   eventually lancinate the willow leaves?

Yes, I was thinking of Simone but also of Camille and Georgette.
After the bath tells me how at 2:00 a.m. waves of rain incite lice
   larvae in the nasal cavity of a red-crowned crane.

Yes, we arrive, returning many times until we find the earth.
You'd think we were ears all along, especially if you examine my
   mouth, empty—as it is—of an action verb.

If you want to contact me, you have at least two options.
Phone me at home by dialing your shoe size combined with
   mine—which may or may not be true—or sleep with more than
   two, but less than four, guinea fowl tucked safely beneath the
   sheet.

A Plague Rat Carrying Calamity Becomes a Panic-Making Horse

If I can get you to hear my voice I will have lived free of disease.
Thus, the translation is conciliatory.

Yes, it is November—the time of harvest animals and moons,
    minutes of increasing sleep.
Is there a deficit of noise in the banditry of seasonal rebellion?

If I can get myself to speak, I will have silenced every article except
    a and *the*.
Chinese geomancers—from simply thrown rock—determine when
    disciples from the rodent north cross into the southern deaths of
    the heart.

A day later, it was, of course, a day later.
Even with geography, months are like that. Many months too.

The only place of solace is the inner noise.
This is not in any way true from this lamp forward, till moons do
    we part.

There are many clichés when it comes to simple things like plague,
    calamity, and rats.
What causes panic for one may stitch the wrist of the softly
    bleeding other.

I decided to move to the mountains and dig a ditch around my tiny
    thatched hut, allowing only marsupials and rats to eat from my
    hand.
There was no water in the West, no rain in the bamboo root, so I
    improvised with night soil as a line of mind.

A Once-Flourishing Pain

A history of sadness is not a bad thing.
I spent one entire lifetime ferrying fighting worms across the
    Mekong Delta.

I do not admit shame. I won't accept your accusation of curried
    coleslaw.
What I left of myself was shredded in Chinese cabbage fields
    absorbing rain.

When a unique jealousy adopts a posture of optimism, coffee is
    rarely persuasive.
I heard the bleeding from a rhinoceros hoof invade even the acacia
    blossom.

For such an earnest commitment, merriment was a far-reaching
    consequence.
A once-flourishing pain suddenly belonged to several of us,
    simultaneously, in our separate caves, as if by blood-stars
    mapped in the afterlife.

Might the diehard moon invade more than my vein?
If it floated belly-down through the mucky Mekong, on what mud
    stick might it snag?

Deliberate speechifying involves a preposterous abuse.
Poems that proclaim aspire to nothing.

It is like going to war to further wrong every wrong.
The opposite of a freezing winter can be a freezing winter.

Our Smallest, Most Tender Selves

Given the exactitude of the knife, I might kneel as moonlight does
    in the pygmy possum's ear.
The brain of the fire ant is extraordinarily complex for such a tiny
    organ.

Hear my treed self singe? My marsupial-my? My how-can-this-be?
I am beside myself with the threat of finally growing up into this
    thing called forgiveness.

Without apparent discomfort, we become friends across the Gobi
    of the chest.
We might be dust mites together, absorbing oily secretions from
    one another's words.

Under a wide range of circumstances, we might be alive.
We might sweeten the human taste, collect star charts from the
    chest cavity of a moldering crow.

The edge of the road is very near a great response.
Enormous depth is wherever we look out and see further inside
    than ever before.

Bathtub Oils and Historical Bones

Two exhausted hemispheres summer-train the night.
I hear the hyena cowl crawl the high dirt and realize I've been alone
  sixty-five years.

I turn to Hernández. I pause for Paz.
I annul the piano dirge of Nicanor Parra's hernia.

I realize the inguinal zone of livid camel water trusts the hazy oasis
  plum.
I extract my ear and hand it back to Van Gogh's accountant.

The largest obsession of selfish concentration was a mathematical
  fulfillment.
I realize I've never been alone among the long rows and tables—
  not even among the probabilities of strict animal milk.

I might be buried in bathtub oils of historical bones.
I might try them on, one by one, and dream Aesop's horse.

I cannot see the spare change in your weeping.
You spend yourself and tell me a fricative seems like a pleasant
  enough gasp.

And so I turn to Desnos and invoke the sleep medicines.
I crawl my Breton, even my Daumal, into the speckled skin at the
  lip of my midnight cup of cinnamon and boiled milk.

An Impossible Immediate Self

It is important to next consider the shade of a limp.
Then point to an ecstatic twelfth-century desert father with a stone
in his mouth at noon.

Sometimes a luxury deadline is merely a hectic context.
Balzac, Chekhov, and Tolstoy jumped to the conclusion of an
impossible immediate self.

But is it impossible, this cheerful conversation between discreet
windows?
How long have I suffered the suffused threat of abandonment,
even now at the transparency of age sixty-five?

It was moonrise in each popularized body part.
An extension of my language continued to fathom the depth of
tortoise swallow among the Trobriand Islands.

I could say, *Translate the dictionary into the damp pavement of a Paris
winter.*
I might mean, *The croup of a gauzy goldfish is neutralized in water.*

Like a broken arm among peanut shells on a tavern floor, the
possibilities of language are bent with proteins.
Suddenly, a complete contemplation—from inside out—of my
many wounds, the seeming sways of salt.

They're really nothing special, I realized.
*But float them downriver in a bark canoe with a damp-dead rat. Like it or
not, they belong solely to me.*

But I Never Would

When we got Asian dogs, we expanded to a king-size bed.
This is what the percolator seemed to slurp, grinding its sloshy
    morning grit.

The most beautiful love is alive, lifetime to lifetime.
I heard this, just as I woke to the fierce strutting of crows.

I know you don't believe everything I write, how many times I've
    died.
How the belly plankton becomes you. How our bodies in heat both
    crave salt.

I respect your blindness as I might the mail carrier's slumped
    shoulder.
I greet her each morning so that she knows she carries something
    alive.

I could kill a summer swan, carve one layer of tender yellow fat as a
    delicacy, and contemplate its swimming *and* its flight.
But I never would—nor *could*—because the swan is sacred
    throughout India.

Please, if you receive this message, pet the dog, expand your hand,
    and replace the bird in your chest one worm at a time. Date this
    message forward three cat lifetimes from now.
Consider this. What year that would be—whether you'll be born
    again screaming or weeping. Weeping or just simply alive.

A Dependent Compassion for
Your Scar

Marsupial Mouth Movements

And inner was the world the way a people talk fast.
Hand me a mask and requisite the sleep I set out in search of the
    pouch.

The inner lives of owls consist of certain parasites designed to
    thrive.
If the Tasmanian tapeworm goes extinct, where does that leave our
    hands as we grasp a photo of the long-gone thylacine?

Little marsupial wolf hunted to extinct. Burn these long ears of
    regret.
Once you're struck into flesh, you find it difficult to hear anything
    that sounds remotely human.

I was suddenly grown up, wearing a crewneck, convincing myself it
    was a cardigan.
I needed a way out of even the toughest sentence, so I ever after a
    new speak.

And inner was that world the bled the people the talk.
So private was my eye, the pineal gland was soggy with
    remembrance. Little beautiful birth-sores full of clarified milk
    and long journeys of the fur.

Rasa

Were my boy-crease aware of the dictionary of birds, then we
   might intersect one another's sleep apnea as if it were ascent.
For far too long now I have been mounted on the wall, stuffed in
   the mouth with particles of Brahms.

He kept birds in his baton to make the oboe flutter.
Before each concert he'd distribute to the orchestra a jacket of sea
   salt, asking no one to wear it so as to release the rhythmic
   wingbeats of the birds.

There is a sinking in my chest whenever the new weather.
I realize it is just the bend of a heavily dozing sunflower, but still I
   shuffle through conjugations of the phrase, *the weighty slur of my
   birth*.

The dictionary of burrs rides me from below.
I am often saddle-sore, just in touching the etymology of my own
   signature.

I looked at the wall until I saw a nail nailed into a nail.
If you can, hand me the stillness of a peacock flying through its
   own death.

Tell me, if you must, where I might find the full flavor of sitar
   music, of a Tagore poem in Bengali, of a peacock's unfulfilled
   cry at dusk.
In which page of the book of large words does it lie, and where did
   I go wrong?

Gobi Noon

So the cave issues forth as if a Shakespeare of red clay.
So the alkali flats flatten out more than all the body's salt.

We recognized our illicit longing and fled to the desert as if we
    were a patriarchal myth.
We journeyed to Qiān fó dòng—Caves of the Thousand
    Buddhas—and sought our body scars embedded in the walls.

Carved, as if alive, the unique quality of sand in the mouth reminds
    us of the rougher textures of love.
Touch the cheek of a woman and beg your past lives, in sequence,
    to survive.

Sure, someone suggested the unfolding of an accordion door and,
    on an outer door, a heavy wooden clapper.
But we were in the desert with nothing but scorched air and a
    memory of quiet sorrow.

In the wider desert gauge of humid affairs, we might exchange the
    axle of a donkey cart for a woman's braid.
Talk is like that, moving in and out of the full frailty of another,
    awaiting the saltily imagined craving of the rain. Calculated.
    Complete. Confused. Complete.

Already-Breathed Air

Now we examine the jazz of the sax. We take our pulse.
We relinquish our pain. We sever one another's frenum.

I ask the exact lines of a book if my name is *George, Georgina*, or
    Giorgia.
I spread an impromptu secret about myself across town and
    intentionally include a mistake.

What if we declined a disruptive gesture?
What if we experienced tortoise talk for what it did to time?

I have buried so much offspring in bruised sand I can no longer
    breathe the waves.
I welcome myself to the described logic of Khlebnikov's clavicle, to
    Vallejo's spleen.

You say you hear a ratchet of already-breathed air.
That it has wrenched up a brilliant pose is more than you can
    strain.

Pull up a table, my friend, and lean further into my ear.
If you talk tenderly and with kitchen clutch, you'll be able to hear
    the entire commotion.

The Blood of the Poet

So the psychoid Christ was there in jongleur Jungian delight.
William Everson recited the absence of his father into each of the
blood oranges he peeled at the sink.

So the idea of a painful valve plagued Vallejo's cheekbone.
And a running sap told César even he had to die, alone in Paris,
without a suit.

So three wives weren't enough to excise his mother's menstrual
scent from the hairs on his chest, which resembled sun sprouts
of unfinished love.
Yes, André Breton became a swan for four, maybe five, days a
month.

Sometimes Miguel Hernández's tuberculous ghost flowed more
freely than others.
Sometimes the Lorca grave trench-lips the chest, as we are all
bitten into the body.

So let us count how many fascist detention camps can fit onto the
head of a quill pen on the island of Samos.
Let us recognize that house arrest for Yannis Ritsos never involved
the playing of cards, nor goat-shots of ouzo in retsina wind.

Rejoice in the sphygmoid blood, the deliriousness of the gnat, the
full-bellied bloat of a mosquito drugged by the sag of torn
African bednets.
The blood of the poet, body to body, mouth to mouth, persists.

Ever Broken

Delicate letters in the hide of an ass.
Delicate math your mouth modulates into mine.

Divert me to the static of your understanding.
Let me form a parrot from these gloves and dust, mimic cage-
strange mouth movements of almost-music.

Repeat after me, *Nothing is worth repeating.*
I'm not talking river risk but the border of a bygone shoulder-slope
of hope.

You say, *Stand at the wall and let the leeches profit from what you should
have said.*
You say, *Gentlemen, aim low, please, and forgive his groinal moan.*

Blindfold me. Forego the smoke. And—yes—keep reading me the
urine inscriptions of Vallejo, even as I stink.
I have been a cartridge echo a long time, afraid of rifles,
slaughterhouses, false teeth, and the one true word I should
have said just once, on one occasion, in the opening suture of
the first page of the first book ever broken.

Mantra Diksha

I have been praying a long time.
This is my resolve—if need be, to get down on all fours and chew
the carpet apart in search of the elusive pineal gland.

Dog-eared pages remind me where we might return.
Once—approximately sixty-four years, ten months, three days, and
seventeen hours ago—we were young.

I fell into your hair the way a planet regains composure.
I'd been circling the flock, biting at their heels, hoping I would find
myself worthy.

Still, it was the wandering that kept me beyond the border of my
own bread.
In the cold, the air reminds me of clear yeasty thought.

We need to sponsor a symposium called *The Pre-Colonial Discovery of
the Preterit.*
Conjugate, for me, my grief spasms, but you may not use my
possible mouth.

You may use me in whatever way you bleed, even if my syntax
slips—especially, then, and though and so.
This is my resolve, my mantra diksha, my get-down-on-all-fours-if-
need-be-and-beckon-broken-plates-of-the-moon—to round
myself out, to sound me toward dissolve.

To Consider Our Milk

I've been visited by an entire farm of sleep.
I place folded hands across my chest, breathe the phrase, *You have
     been truly touched.*

A bone sutra is a liniment of skeletal chalk?
We cry for milk. The book grows wet, stains our mouth.

If it had a chest, my small intestine would feel your softest kiss.
Somehow it does, and I grow calm in a room without turning
     mirrors.

To even consider a swan-necked number makes me detect a galaxy
     in horse droppings and gnats.
We're all alike because of the single spinal nerve.

Massage the medulla oblongata. Feel starlight inhabit each
     incarnate moan.
Ligaments of forest trees might be *willow root* or *frankincense-my-
     mouth.*

I can't stop chalking my own framed cage.
I have been insisted by an arm, a sheep, a consigned clutch.

Somehow all the plants and their glorious breathings know my
     name.
Tell me, but keep it brief. Is it *You? Me? Us?*

Buffalo Jump

On the inside of my body it is written, *He watched a cliff called a*
    buffalo jump and imagined.
Turn my tongue inside out, and you will inscribe a private, forested
    cluster.

I come to you in secret when you most bleed.
For four, maybe five, weeks a month, I am full inside your fullness
    as if your hips.

If I had not developed this rash for you, I would be left dissecting
    a moth of all its moon-bleed.
If you had not counted to eight, had not worn that short denim
    skirt, I would have never known how my dreaming.

Please, tell Henri I much prefer his prose poems to the translation
    of my wrist.
Tell him it's the block of sand, the pin oak, the impenetrable forest
    that grants me safe.

Yes, I am happily married and beg you not to bend over to pick up
    the papers in that way.
I cannot be held responsible for what they might say.

A Dependent Compassion for Your Scar

I could change if my oblique self divulged a dependent compassion
    for your scar.
The raccoon family is back, gifting through my present state of
    trash.

I will contact the cartographer.
I will buy his supper with my bones.

We might voice a misplaced plea.
The fly in our soup may actually be part of the seasoning for the
    stew.

Sometimes a cigar is just now lit.
The smoke of what I thought you were thinking does indeed stink.

Mark my mouth with lime.
Mark my boundary with a word as delicious as *terrera*.

No Here but Now

Across the coalsack of my mind, every dead Java sparrow, every
shape of green.
Until the opium turn stopped, Saturn believed its rings could
wobble-on forever.

So that now, much obliged, the field mice gnaw the bones of a
fallen owl.
So that now, the greedy grubs knock heads at the blistering carcass
with a weight only the grass knows.

Up the mountain, there is another mountain.
I have been pickaxing my brain for a place of peace for sixty-five
years.

If I stuck up for myself, finally told those who hurt me that they
were wrong, would it be me or the field mice who would
spontaneously combust?
Would I travel a long time in the brain ways of a dying owl, as if I
was a fleck of sky never quite peeled apart and entered?

Tell me how we can fit our complete animal into the constant of
one another's sorrow.
There is no *there* but *here*, no *here* but *now*, no *now* but *always*.

Great and Awful and Gifts Us

Has the voice done any injury?
Has the peacock color of our harm redeemed us?

I have traveled from here to there and now find myself back home
    in a good wool shirt.
Yes, it snowed in both places, but pieces of bread refused the ache
    of raisins falling apart from the stem.

Burn the bamboo. Familiar your voice. Ask yourself out to death.
Gossip among the faraway cactus thorn, placing your entire vowel
    down upon a bet on the silkworm they hung to dry.

In less than it takes the color green there is a desert past foretold.
Tonight's sleep predicts all the dry mouths it is predicated upon.

This is all happening because it is supposed to.
Yes, there was a crow injured in Kansas, but we managed its
    feather count in Nebraska.

Foragers fade away slowly, the way foragers do.
The voice is great and awful and gifts us the calm stormy tail of a
    peacock proclaiming—over and again in that peculiar Bengali
    shriek—*It is dusk, it is dusk, and the eggs are bled by our own
    over-anxious mouths.*

The Methods of Production

A long transparent maneuver flattens the weight of woven rain.
Or, *A maneuvered transport weaves flat heavy storms.*

Now I come to translating myself.
Steep a pot of oolong tea. I am excruciating myself in your spleen.

A man or a woman, in general, could be a rich history, a soiled
    linguistic itch.
Especially if we speak of *controlling the methods of production*, we must
    tax the wedding bed, or the kitchen chair she straddles you on,
    or the psalm-said of her breast.

Wrap your legs around my hips as if the tightening mattered.
Say, *your stain, your stain*, over and again into my mouth, so that I
    might release the owl's midnight resin.

We belly-touch the whalebone washed up between us into a vast
    sestina.
I have been repeating seven—not six—words my entire life, one
    for each chakra.

It *does* matter. *All* of it matters.
OM, Belovèd. OM, Belovèd. OM, Belovèd. OM.

NOTES

The epigraphs are drawn from Robert Paddle, *The Last Tasmanian Tiger: The History and Extinction of the Thylacine*, Cambridge University Press, 2000, and from César Vallejo, *The Complete Posthumous Poetry*, translated by Clayton Eshleman and José Rubia Barcia, University of California Press, 1978.

The phrase in "Angora," *"Conditions are always neutral,"* refers to a concept often repeated in various ways by Paramahansa Yogananda throughout his teachings, including one paraphrase by Swami Kriyananda, "Objective conditions and all events and circumstances are always neutral. It is how you react to them that makes you sad or happy." *The Essence of Self-Realization: The Wisdom of Paramhansa Yogananda* [*sic*]. Recorded, compiled and edited by Swami Kriyananda, Crystal Clarity Publishers, 1990.

"Tying the Traveling Man to the Tree of Soul" takes its title from, and was written after, a watercolor by the Indian artist, Gopikrishna, to accompany a reproduction of this artwork in *International Gallerie: A Journal of Ideas* (Mumbai, India), Volume 13, Number 2, 2010.

"Longing in the Grand Grassland" takes its title from, and was written after, a piece of instrumental music appearing on *Working Out of the Western Pass*, Di, Ba-wu & Xun Master: Li Chen, conducted by Zhang Lieh and performed in association with the Ensemble of the Shensi Songs & Dances Theatre. Chinese Dragon Records, Inc. / Janus Resource International Co., Ltd. This particular song was composed by Ning Pa-Sheng and Li Chen in 1986.

Stanza four of "Gold" refers to and modifies part of the title of an Elspeth Huxley book, *The Flame Trees of Thika: Memories of an African Childhood*, William Morrow and Company, 1959.

The title of "Placental Chauvinism" pays homage to a term Robert Paddle describes in *The Last Tasmanian Tiger: The History and Extinction of the Thylacine* (cited in an earlier note above).

"A Plague Rat Carrying Calamity Becomes a Panic-Making Horse" takes its title from a chapter gloss in *The Travels of Lao Ts'an*, by Liu T'ieh-yun, translated by Harold Shadick, Columbia University Press, 1990.

"The Blood of the Poet" borrows its title from a William Everson book, *The Blood of the Poet: Selected Poems*, Broken Moon Press, 1994, and it makes a nod to the Jean Cocteau film, with a slightly different title, *The Blood of a Poet* (*Le Sang d'un Poète*); the line, "So the idea of a painful valve plagued Vallejo's cheekbone," refers to Vallejo's line, "and what an idea of a painful valve in his cheekbone!" from his untitled poem, beginning, "Idle on a stone," from César Vallejo, *The Complete Posthumous Poetry*, cited in the first note on the previous page.

ABOUT THE AUTHOR

George Kalamaras, former Poet Laureate of Indiana (2014-2016), is the author of eleven full-length books of poetry and seven poetry chapbooks. He has received several national prizes for his poetry, and he spent several months in India in 1994 on an Indo-U.S. Advanced Research Fellowship. He is Professor of English at Purdue University Fort Wayne (formerly Indiana University-Purdue University Fort Wayne), where he has taught since 1990. He lives with his wife, writer Mary Ann Cain, and their beagle, Bootsie, in Fort Wayne, Indiana.

www.ingramcontent.com/pod-product-compliance
Lightning Source LLC
Chambersburg PA
CBHW022159080426
42734CB00006B/503